Be a Confident Woman

Naomi Elm

ACKNOWLEDGMENTS

To my wonderful husband who supports me. You have encouraged me and given me reasons to continue to be a confident woman to encourage many women all over the world.

CONTENTS

Imagine being a confident you. Being able to achieve your goals. Suddenly there's an obstacle stopping you from going to the next level.

There are two options. You can decide to break the obstacle, jump over or find a comfortable bed and sleep off. Challenging situations you face are like that obstacle but the good news is that you can survive.

" Love is like a sweet slumber. The deeper you're in love, the more likely you get hurt if it is with the wrong person. It captivates the soul but is hard to break and when you do, it hurts like wounds that take years to heal and when it heals, it leaves scars."

Are you lacking confidence? Have you been worried about your body and the way you feel? This is a message for you.

You will learn:
1.   Identify your weakness and how you can win.
2.   Learn how to realize your purpose and strength.
3.   Learn tips on how to let go of insecurities and build self-confidence.

8

You don't have a Barbie curve."
" Why is your breast saggy?"
"You're nothing."

The world is full of negativity. From the womb, all eyes have been on you. The world wants you out there to show them what you've got. You're not alone. Thousands of people feel that way. Women tend to be the most fragile emotionally. We're recognized as weaker vessels" and as a result, we learn to be confident, strong, and happy. Come with me as we analyze wrong and powerful sentences that make women insecure.

YOU'RE UGLY
"You feel the world is staring at you right now. You feel there is nowhere to hide and at the same time want to hide somewhere peaceful forever. You feel there's a dreamland where it's just you, the cool breeze and flowers but you know it's just a mere dream."

Dear One,

You are not ugly because you are created by a unique God who wants you to be happy. No one can assess you. Do not focus on the world's opinion about outer impressions because they might make us feel that if we don't look a certain way, we are not beautiful. How you feel about yourself is important.

Think about it. Why the word " ugly"? That is because you're uniquely different and wonderfully created.

Tip- Be positive.

YOU'RE USELESS

"You wonder why you exist. You question why you live. You place a hand on your head and wonder if you're cursed but at that moment you find no answer."

10

To the most adorable woman,
 Do you want to walk around with your head down? No, that won't happen. Do you know why? Because you're not useless!
You're strong and you haven't realized it yet. You're not useless because God created you for a purpose. There are unavoidable goals in your life and to find these goals, you need to get out of that thought, raise your head high and ask yourself what you want to do and where you want to start.
Tip- Find your true purpose.

YOU ARE FAT
 "You look in the mirror and all you see is fat. You feel sad and wish you could be more attractive. You hide more from people and groups. No outfit seems to satisfy the way you feel about yourself."

Dear special woman,
 To be beautiful doesn't mean you have to look like a particular person. Cherish your body and personality because it shows the real you. There are many things to engage in, happiness to share, and comfort to give others.

Give yourself a treat, change your wardrobe, be friends with the people who love you, pick up a new exercise to relax your nerves, and always smile!
Tip- Love and cherish yourself more

11

YOU HAVE STRETCH MARKS
"You feel disgusted and disappointed. You search for different methods and options to make it disappear. You're scared to open yourself to your husband in the daylight because you're worried he'll scream hysterically and hate you."

Hey beautiful,
 Stretch marks aren't as horrible as you think. You are a unique woman and it's part of you. It shows how extremely beautiful you are. Does your partner detest it? Don't worry! Take deep breaths for it's not the end of the world. Take charge of your life and love yourself. This is who you are! You are not going to feel insecure because he said that rather, you're going to wipe that tears away and get busy with your life. Love yourself, smell different and be confident! Your body is beautiful. Do not worry, your husband will see how stronger you have become. He will love you more and most of all, love you for who you are.

So girl, stop browsing all the remedies you can find and show off your beautiful marks!
Tip- Embrace what makes you, you.

12

YOU'RE AN OLD CARGO
"You smile sadly and wish they could understand how it feels to be weak. You wish you could be strong the way you used to be. You feel solitary and yearn for some company. You want to talk to someone who understands you but you know they're hard to find."

To the most amazing mother,
 You have been through a lot in life. You've been a mother, superwoman, teacher, and many more. You've been a confident and strong woman to face different difficulties, sacrifices, and disappointments with the help of God. Anyone who compares you to an old cargo doesn't understand. You'll always be an unforgettable legend till the end of time.
Tip- You are a graceful woman.

SMALL BREAST
"You tell yourself that you're going to make it bigger than it is someday."

Dear Sis,

I can't help but wonder if you know how stunning you are with those around you and the beautiful gifts God has bestowed on you. Do not feel that possessing a certain look or making your breast bigger will make you feel better because these cravings don't last forever. What last forever is that good

13

heart and kind personality you possess. Think about it. What if women do not have breasts? Cherish those gifts!

Tip- You're wonderfully made.

YOU WILL END UP ALONE

"You feel like running for miles without stopping to take a breath."

Dear Superwoman,
 You can't end up alone because you're not alone in this world. We need you. People need you out there. You may not understand that you possess beautiful qualities in you that could change and save lives until you stay and try. Stay strong and fight your fears because that makes you a confident woman. You are never alone.
Tip- Face your fears.

YOU HAVE NO FUTURE

" You look at the heavens and ask with tears why it happened to you."

Dear wonderful woman,
 No one can decide that. You're full of hope and purpose

14

because you're alive. Start by defining your aspirations, and analyze your skills and resources. Do not give up! Life may be a rough one but you'll find your way out if you're always willing to learn more and fight to survive. Are you ready to fight? Get ready to go to battle because you will win!
Tip- Take charge of your future.

WHY ARE YOU NOT MARRIED?

"Dear Singles,

 You may feel sad when you hear that question. Having a handsome prince with horses from a fairy tale land that brings joy to your life and helps you grow is a wonderful thing. But don't feel pressured to accept anyone because

someone is calculating your life. It takes patience to find a good man. Focus on building your personality while you're still single. Be trustworthy, faithful, reliable, and industrious. Learn to love yourself more because it'll help you to avoid being insecure. Do not feel you have to change your personality when you're dating. Take care of yourself. At the right time, a wonderful man will come to stay.
Tip- Be patient.

15

YOU CAN NOT KEEP A MAN
" You feel hurt when he doesn't love you the way you deeply loved him."

Dear strong woman,
 Have you ever felt something is wrong with you and your relationship with others?
You might feel you don't deserve affection. The truth is, some women with good hearts are married to the wrong men. It doesn't mean they're bad and don't love God. It means they are giving themselves a chance to change themselves and a chance to be better. That is the purpose. So, nothing is wrong with you meeting him. Always know that you're very special.

Tip- You're a special woman.

YOUR MARRIAGE WILL NOT LAST
" Deep in your heart, you feel love so strongly for him. But it hurts when his actions make you feel the opposite."

Dear Confident woman,
 Marriage isn't perfect. No matter how hard you try, problems will always occur. There are times you want to punch him if you can and there are times you want to embrace and kiss him. No matter how you feel, how you deal with each other is important. We are all imperfect and

16

we struggle with our imperfections. Now imagine two imperfect souls coming together. What can help are :
- Putting God first in your marriage.
- Accepting all imperfections and dealing with them.
- Viewing each other as a team.

Putting God first in your marriage.
God is the originator of marriage. He knows you and your husband. Why don't you explain the problems in prayer to him?
Accepting all imperfections and dealing with them. Do not expect perfection from anyone. Learn about each other's likes and dislikes and talk about how to deal with them.
Viewing each other as a team.

When you view each other as a team, tackling problems that arise will be easy. View that problem as the enemy, not your spouse. That way, you're a team. As you spend years together, forgive each other freely and apologize not only when you're wrong. Treat him well when one of you is lacking. Talk about problems with humility. Your marriage shouldn't be a race to win. Learn how to say "sorry" when you're angry. Apologizing and speaking with humility can make the heart fragile. What will you use to quench the flames? Gas? You wouldn't want that. Water is like humble words. When spoken, It softens the heart.

17

YOU DON'T HAVE A SENSE OF FASHION

Dear friend,
You don't have to feel awful when you hear that. You know you can do more if you have the power to do so but right now, you have clean low-cost clothes and that doesn't make you different from anyone.
Do not feel unpleasant if you can't look a certain way at the moment. Growth is about stages. Soon, you will have the chance to acquire anything you need and while you're patient, focus not on what people say about you, but on how you can grow to be a successful human. Remember growth takes time, effort, and patience,
Tip- Growth takes time, effort, and patience.

CHALLENGE YOURSELF. Pleasing others is like going to a lonely war that is not your fight. You don't have to go that far. It is time to stand up and ignore these criticisms. It is impossible to love yourself when you don't have an idea of who you are. Take yourself out, discover, and like. Embrace your imperfections because they're part of what makes you, you. To be loved isn't a bad thing but you have to accept that sometimes people won't like you. Do not waste your time trying to please people. Remember it's like a battle of you alone. Be yourself because that is the easiest way.

Treat Your Body With Respect. The urge to look in the mirror and list out things you hate about your body is common but treating your body with respect can decrease that urge. Take a bubble bath, get a massage and hug people you feel comfortable with.

Appreciate Your Personality. You may find it easy to praise

18

others but struggle to give yourself any thanks and it makes it easy for you to feel down.

- Recognize your good qualities.
- Focus on your strengths.
- Be positive.
- Keep a journal.
- Be kind to others.

Be Open With Your Partner. If you are married, communicating with your partner is one way to express your feelings about insecurity.

If you're a professional hairstylist, check out our hair care and braiding solutions. These can help your hair growth!

To all Confident hairstylists,

I know what you are all thinking.

You're probably thinking about spending too much on expensive shampoos or seeing different pictures of hair solutions that you see on videos but not getting the desired

19

result.

But you won't see pictures. I promise that if you read on, you're going to learn a thing or two that will help your hair grow, maintain your client's hair like a professional hairstylist, and expose you to new methods of hair braiding.
Regular hair care is essential for women of all ages and hair types, whether your hair is relaxer-free hair or not.
Regardless of style, texture, and color, there is one thing every woman wants: Hair that looks healthy. You're not

alone. Every woman wants the same. This is not the time to give up on your hair, resolve it, or stay in bed all day browsing through different hair options. Now is the time to keep reading. This is for you! We've spoken with experts and I assure you it is 100% safe and natural.

• Know what the problem is. Our hair is like what we eat to stay healthy. Just like eating good food, our hair wants the same. So apart from a health issue, our hair should grow healthily.

Now, let us talk about hair types, scalp problems, and solutions.

COMMON HAIR PROBLEMS
Dandruff
Dandruff needs no formal introductions. It's when the skin of the scalp peels off and flakes making the most

attractive hair look horrible. While germs could make dandruff worse, the primary causes are dry scalp and sensitivity to certain products.
Tip: Wash your hair with rice water once every month.

Solutions.
* Moisturize and oil your scalp every three days.
* Add adequate omega-3 acids to your diet.
* Scrub your hair softly when washing.

- Consult your dermatologist before using any product.

Hair Loss.
Oh! That can be very embarrassing.
Losing 5 to 10 strands of hair in a day is normal. If you experience a sudden and noticeable increase in hair loss, it's time to take action.

Solution.
- Steam your hair.
You need these few things after steaming.

Garlic
Ginger
Turmeric powder
Eggs
Coconut water
Moringa powder (optional)

21

How?
- Blend the garlic and ginger, and pour into a bowl.
- Add your eggs (preferably two)
- Add your Tumeric powder and two teaspoons of Moringa powder
- Finally, your coconut water. (one coconut is enough)

- Apply one hour after steaming, cover with a net cap and wash an hour later.
- Do this once in three months.

OILY SCALP

Oily scalp isn't a problem if you ask me. If your hair is oily, no worries! All you need to do is to wash your hair quite often.

Ingredients like lactic acid help regulate the production of oil.

SPLIT ENDS

When oil from the scalp doesn't reach the ends of the hair, they tend to dry and split.

Solutions.

- Trim the weak split ends to keep your hair healthy.
- If your hair is light and soft, stay away from straightening your hair and use other methods to stretch your hair instead.
- Rubbing a dash of oil into your ends can reduce the split appearance while also providing nourishment.

22

- The thicker your hair, the more moisturizing it needs.

Hair Colour Damage.

Do you know that regular coloring sessions can damage your hair?

Whether it's a root touch-up, bleaching, or highlights, coloring your hair all the time can make it brittle. The frequent chemicals can also cause dryness, dullness, and breakage.

If you've colored your hair, you need to give it extra care and attention.

Solutions.

•	Make sure you steam every month, you can follow the " before steaming secrets" on the previous page.

•	Wash your hair with a soft shampoo and conditioner.

YOUR HAIRBRUSH AND YOU

Imagine yourself working all day and on your way home, you tell yourself you need a warm bath. At home, you turn on the shower and wet your hair. Then suddenly someone offered to help you brush your hair as you scrub your body.

23

How would you feel?

Oh my!

You don't need to tell.

Brushing our hair has more benefits and some of the benefits of brushing our hair include:

- Improves our hair health.

When brushing your hair, the distribution of healthy oil happens which gives your hair a nice glow.

- Increases blood flow.

Brushing your hair is like giving yourself a thorough massage. Do you notice when someone brushes your hair you feel sleepy? So, brush your hair thoroughly without worry!

HOW TO PROTECT YOUR CORNROWS Cornrows are ways to show how naturally beautiful you can look. While these styles are unique, you might be worried about how they will look next week.

Here are some ways to keep your cornrow nourished and comfortable.

Make It Comfortable.

Do not tie or style your hair too tight. Tie your hair as loosely as you can.

Moisturize your Cornrow.

Cornrows are a popular option for those seeking to reduce frequent hair styling and maintenance.

Natural moisturizing prevents dryness and scalp conditions such as dandruff.

Tip: Ask your hairstylist to start with your natural hair. Avoid starting your cornrow with hair extensions to prevent hair loss.

If your hair is thin and soft, check out loose styles you can do that suit your hair type.

Before steaming Tips.

Let's be honest with each other. Steaming has its benefits such as repairing damaged hair.

As we've learned so far, there are instances where your hair is trying to pass a message to you. Why don't you try steaming first?

Benefits

•   Steaming opens your hair cuticle which allows new ones to grow.

•   It prevents dandruff and hair loss.

•   Improves your hair texture.

What to do after steaming?

Don't rush to wash anything. Wait until your hair is cool to the touch.

Tip: An hour after steaming, you can apply your mixed eggs, Turmeric, Moringa, garlic, and ginger. For fantastic results, do not wash immediately after applying.

HAIR BRAIDING SECRETS

Shh…do not tell anyone I am about to reveal some secrets to you. Learning how to braid hair is simpler said than done. Every hair stylist knows that. Even braids that are supposed to be easy seem to require some sort of superman strength.

But, no worries. Stay with me as I share deep secrets that can make you more professional in braids. The general braids we know are called loose braids and anyone can do them. But, the one I'm going to reveal is a tight neat braid.

Step by Step to Tight braid Rule.

- Straighten your hands.
- Stay where you are, the braid will shift.
- Make your crossing stronger and tighter.

Now practice before you move on.

The most important rule is:

26

Stay where you are, the braid will shift. As you braid, do not shift your hands down too quickly to get to the end. Where are you rushing to? Remember this is tight, not loose. Let the braid do the job.

Why tight Braids?
- Lasts longer.
- Looks outstanding and elegant.
- Adds a niche to your work.

Do you know?
Tight braids do not cause hair loss.
As you braid, trim immediately. Practice more and see what you can do!
How about twists?

HAIR TWIST SECRET METHOD

After dividing the section of hair, whether you're a left twister or right twister, follow these steps to achieve a different and neat twist.
- After parting the section you want to work on, braid the hair a little and use your pin to pass the extension.
- If you're attaching extensions, conceal the real hair using the extension before you twist.
- When you twist, do not simply cross each section

of hair. Twist the hair three times before crossing. It will give you a neat finish.

Twist three times before crossing

As you twist, do not twist the way you know. Make sure you conceal the hair and twist the hair three times before you cross it. Repeat over and over again to the end.
I don't say practice makes perfect. I would say practice makes it look good or makes it work.
So, practice!

Why?

- Last longer.
- Adds a niche to your work.

Note: As you twist, trim immediately.

CORNROW SECRETS.

Cornrows are interesting, beautiful, and practical ways to

28

look different. They add style to your looks and protect your hair.

We all know that before you start braiding, you may want to add a bit of edge control to make it more appealing.

For someone more experienced with cornrow, we are going to learn new ways to add to your methods.

*   Make your hands straight as you weave.

*   Do not hurry to the finish line. Stay where you are and weave, the cornrow will shift itself.

*   Be aware of the two sides, your left hand and your right.

*   Slowly detangle the hair when tangled to prevent bent cornrow.

*   Start with natural hair if you're using hair extensions.

Do not hurry to the finish line, stay where you are.

The urge to finish quickly is common. But to achieve beautiful cornrows, you have to slow down. Staying where you are and leaving the job to your cornrow will do.

START WITH THE NATURAL HAIR IF YOU'RE USING AN EXTENSION

This is very important. Hairs that are not carefully picked before an extension are risky, they can lead to hair loss.

Note: Make sure you oil or moisturize the hair before you start.

29

questions? You're welcome!

Coming soon. Check out our new books. The Red-haired.

Pursuit of love.

About the author

Naomi Elm is a writer. When she's not writing, she spends most of her time reading and encouraging confident women.

www.ingramcontent.com/pod-product-compliance
Lightning Source LLC
Chambersburg PA
CBHW020947160726
47993CB00007B/2976